# MORE

### DO MORE OF WHAT MATTERS MOST AND DISCOVER THE LIFE OF YOUR DREAMS

## MICHAEL LISTER

Copyright © 2021 by Michael Lister

All rights reserved.

No part of this book may be reproduced in any form or by any electronic or mechanical means, including information storage and retrieval systems, without written permission from the author, except for the use of brief quotations in a book review.

*For Denise, whose idea this was.*

# THANK YOU

A very special thanks for invaluable contributions and support goes to: Denise Denaro, LaDonna Diaz, Jill Mueller, Vanessa Serio.

# THE MORE GUIDED JOURNAL

Don't miss the MORE Guided Journal

# THE MEANING SERIES

MORE is part of the Meaning Series by Michael Lister. Check out the other informative and inspirational titles today.

# PART ONE
# MINDSET, MOTIVATION, AND MEANING

# ONE

**You can do more of what matters most!**

You can do more of what matters most. Starting right now. I can show you how.

No matter how productive you are now, you can do more. But not just more—*more* of what truly matters most.

Make a list of what really matters most to you.

I know you don't want to. I know you want to keep reading. But humor me and make the stupid list.

Be honest. Delve deep. Don't write down what you think you're supposed to say.

**WHAT MATTERS MOST** to me is:

_____
_____
_____
_____
_____
_____

Look at your list. Were you honest? If you were, then these are the things you want to do more of, have more time with, invest more in, become better at, maximize your effectiveness and efficiency in. So let's talk about how to do just that.

# TWO

## Do you ever sleep?

I HAVE A FULL, rich, meaningful, fun life. But not just any life. The life I want. My dream life.

For a while now, my friends and family have marveled at my productivity. Okay, maybe not *marveled*. Maybe more like noticed and occasionally commented on. But still. And they've encouraged me to write a book about it—well, at least a few of them have.

Over the years, I've often been asked—especially in the context of the number of books I've written and how full my life is—"Do you ever sleep?"

The answer is *I do*. I sleep plenty—well, at least enough. Or nearly enough most of the time.

The thing is, every time someone comments on my productivity, I think about many, many ways I could get more done. My productivity is in continuous need of improving, tweaking, editing, altering. So this is first and foremost a book I'm writing to and for me—not because I'm Mr. Productivity but because I aspire to be.

Still, it's fair to say I get a lot done. And do so consistently. And have for most of my adult life.

But it's not just a lot of work I get done. It's a lot of fun too—a lot of family-and-friends time. Because I believe our best, most productive lives involve productivity and balance in every area of our lives—of which work is only a small part.

Before we go any further, let's define what we mean by productivity. A basic definition of productivity is the state or quality of producing something; the effectiveness of productive effort as measured in terms of the rate of output per unit of input; the quality, state, or fact of being able to generate, create, enhance, or bring forth something.

Productivity is the practice of creating and generating the quality and quantity of our lives. It's as simple and complex as what and how much we do with the gift of our lives.

I'm not a trained productivity expert—if there is such a thing—not some sort of guru. I'm just a boy standing in front of a girl asking her to love him—no wait, asking her to love her life and get the most out of it. I'm a man who woke up to the sacredness and brevity of life. I'm someone who, in order to make the most out of life, has implemented some productivity practices that work for me. In that way, this is sort of what could be called the Michael Method. What follows is my own unique, idiosyncratic hacks and habits, tips and tricks for being productive. I believe you'll find that most of these practices and techniques will work for you. Use the ones that do. Disregard those that don't. And with the ones that do, tailor them to fit your life, your needs. Come up with variations and iterations that best suit you.

As a novelist, I've produced over forty books in twenty-seven years—while raising a family and being an extremely involved dad, maintaining close relationships with loved ones and friends, doing charity work, pursuing spiritual growth and self-development, and alongside exercise, social gatherings, music, creativity, adventures, and lots and lots of fun.

It's not just the quantity of novels I've produce that's commented on but the quality too. And it's not just the quantity of what I pack into my days but the quality of my life that I get asked about. My desire for and commitment to the work I do is not just to produce a high volume of work, but a high level of quality. This recent review from *Publisher's Weekly* about my long-running John Jordan mystery series says it all: "Lister's strong 24th John Jordan novel expertly balances emotion and detection while doling out logical, gut-wrenching twists. This series shows no signs of losing steam." There is much to like in this review, but my favorite part is the recognition that after twenty-four books in the same series, it's still going strong and shows no signs of losing steam. Quantity *and* quality is the goal. My desire and commitment for my life is not just to cram a great deal into it but to fill it with a ton of what really matters, with what makes for a quality life worth living. There's no trade review journal for life the way there is for publishing, but when those closest to you tell you how much they appreciate your priorities and the way you consistently care for them and others, it's the life equivalent of a 5-star review. And my goal for you is exactly the same. My deep desire is for this book to assist you in creating both the quantity and quality of work and life you deeply desire.

So I share this with you not as someone who studied productivity at university or is a consultant for Fortune 500 companies, but merely as a man who has consistently been productive, and what I'm sharing with you is what has worked for me. I believe that many of the techniques and approaches I share will also work for you, but for each one, you will need to tailor it to fit your needs, your personality, your lifestyle. Each of us can be more productive than we are right now, myself included, and what I am sharing in this book will help you and help me do that. Be that. Become that. These are reminders to help us remember what matters most. These are examples and techniques and lifestyle choices and approaches to help us each achieve our goals.

# THREE

**Do Something**

AS WITH ALL things that matter, we don't need to just talk about it. We need to *be* about it.

Talking is important and helpful. You should read every word of this book, talk to others about it, think about them, reflect on them, but all toward one end—and that is to put them into practice. To actually *do* them.

There's a real danger in talking about things, reading about things, listening to others talk or teach about things. We can fool ourselves into thinking that we've done something. Listening isn't doing. Reading isn't doing. We haven't truly learned something until we do it, until we put it into consistent practice in our lives.

So before we go any further, do something. Do something productive right now.

NOW!

Get up off your ass and accomplish something.

Look back at your list of what matters most to you. Pick something and do it.

Want a better relationship with your spouse, child, parents, coworker? Reach out to them right now. Shoot them a text asking about their day. Give them a quick call and express care and concern.

Want a deeper, more meaningful, spiritual life? Take a few moments and meditate.

Want to be thinner, healthier, more fit? Get up right now and move around. Stretch. Do some cardio. Lift some weights. Pull up an exercise video and, well, exercise.

Want to be better at the instrument you play? Pick it up right now and play it. Put in some practice. Right now.

Want to know more, be smarter, more educated? Pull up a Ted Talk on a topic you're interested in and listen to it right now.

Do something now. I'll wait. I'm not going anywhere.

You can return to this book once you've done something. I will be here waiting for you.

WHAT CAN you do right now that will increase your productivity, give you a sense of accomplishment, cause you to have less on your to-do list later?

_____
_____
_____
_____
_____
_____

# WHAT ARE YOU WAITING FOR?

# FOUR

**Memento Mori**

YOU'RE RUNNING LATE.

The memorial service is already underway when you slip into the back of the small, old, creaky church and take a seat on the back pew.

The priest tasked with conducting the funeral service stands behind the lectern on the platform, seeming to hover over the open casket on the lower level before him. After his earlier awkward comments, he grows more calm and confident as he begins the eulogy.

You lean forward slightly and tilt your head, trying to make out what he's saying.

What kind of life did the poor bastard have? What did he do with his days?

Your attention drifts away a moment and when it returns, the priest is talking about who the man loved and who loved him.

And then onto his accomplishments—the this and that, the interests and activities that he spent his time and his resources, in other words, his life, on.

Wait, what did he just say? Say that again. That can't be right. Can it? How is that possible?

You realize with a jarring jolt that shakes you to your core that the poor bastard he's talking about is you.

Glancing down at the casket, you confirm that it is indeed you. Somehow, some way, you have been allowed to attend your own funeral, and after the initial shock and denial, you realize what a gift it is. You get to see and hear what your life meant, what it amounted to, what you did with it. You get a very vivid memento mori.

The Latin phrase *memento mori* means something like "remember to die" or "remember that you are mortal" or "be reminded death is your destination."

For me, the best and wisest considerations and contemplations of productivity, of what we're going to do with our lives, begins at the end, with our deaths.

Your days are numbered. What are you going to do with them?

The time to contemplate your eulogy or your memorial service is not at the end of your life, but as early and as often as you can. Beginning with the end in mind, having some sense of your destination before you start your journey ensures that you'll head in the right direction. Our paths are defined by where we're headed.

Being productive, doing the most of what matters most with our lives begins with us contemplating the end.

Set your trajectory. Let your death, your sacred, precious, limited life be the star by which you steer.

Let the fragility of life and the finality of death provide you with focus and clarity. Memento mori is a call to life, to carpe diem—it's a plea from beyond the grave to live before it's too late.

Don't put off important things until later. Later is always too late.

Make yourself a reminder, a memento mori.

Remember to die. Remember to live.

Take a moment right now and write a draft of your obituary. What do you want to have accomplished? What do you most want to be known for?

Write it down now. Let it be your guiding star. Begin living your best death now.

## MY OBITUARY:

---------------------------------------------------------------
---------------------------------------------------------------
---------------------------------------------------------------
---------------------------------------------------------------
---------------------------------------------------------------
---------------------------------------------------------------

# FIVE

**Productivity with Purpose**

PURPOSEFUL PRODUCTIVITY IS NOT JUST about getting more done but about getting more out of life. It's about doing what matters most and living our best lives possible.

I have become convinced through my experience that the most meaningful life is the most productive one—but productive in the ways that matter most, productive in ways that give us more meaning, fulfill our purpose, and enable us to be of benefit to others. When we are productive in the areas that really matter, we make the lives of those around us better. We make the world a better place.

This is productivity with a purpose. This is the act of developing our gifts, our talents, and living according to our purposes and callings in such a way that we not only benefit ourselves but uplift, inspire, and help others. My deep desire is to evolve, to become, to grow, to develop in order that I might fulfill my purpose, live my best life possible, *and* enhance the lives of others.

The Persian poet Rumi said, "Be a lamp, or a lifeboat, or a ladder. Help someone's soul heal. Walk out of your house like a shepherd." In doing so, in being a shepherd to lost sheep, in being a healer to hurt souls, we find the true purpose of our lives, gifts, callings. It's not enough for us to be gifted, to identify, invest in, and become proficient with our gifts. After doing all this we must then give them away. A big part of the purpose of our gifts is to help and heal others by sharing them.

Anything less than this is selfishness and self-centered. Self-development isn't the end, but the means to an end. It's actually the beginning. We invest in ourselves because we matter, and we uncover and invest in our experiences, gifts, and talents in order to share them with the world. And by sharing our experiences, gifts, and talents with the world, our lives have more meaning. This is the mindset of meaningful productivity. It's not about busyness or addiction or distractions, but purpose, meaning, and fulfillment.

The great transcendentalist thinker and philosopher Ralph Waldo Emerson said, "The purpose of life is not to be happy. It is to be useful, to be honorable, to be compassionate, to have it make some difference that you have lived and lived well." I would just add that being useful, honorable, and compassionate leads to a happy, meaningful, purposely productive life.

Whether it's our most ancient wisdom traditions or the latest peer-reviewed study, those in the know teach us that there are four essential areas we need to focus our attention on to achieve our best, most productively meaningful lives. I will explore and expand on each throughout this book, but I want to list them here so you can see them, read them, ingest them, burn them into your brain.

For our very best, most fulfilling lives, we each need to work toward achieving:

1. Health—physical, mental, emotional, and spiritual well-being.
2. Socialization—a sense of belonging, a sense of contributing, a sense of being seen.
3. Satisfaction—the opportunity to do what we love and enjoy.
4. Transcendence—a sense of the sacred, of spirituality, of ineffability, of connection with that which is beyond us.

For me, life is a precious, sacred gift—to be respected and honored, appreciated and cherished. I certainly see the point of view of those who see it differently, who believe it's "a tale told by an idiot, full of sound and fury, signifying nothing," and I even sympathize with their perspective. But I'm convinced it's far, far more than that. I agree with psychologist and Holocaust survivor Viktor Frankl that life is meaningful—or can be. To me, the search for meaning makes life meaningful. It's my intention to get the most out of my life, to live a life worthy of the gift of the life I've been given.

As Agatha Christie famously said, "I have sometimes been wildly, despairingly, acutely miserable . . . but through it all I still know quite certainly that just to be alive is a grand thing."

Life is limited. I have a finite number of days, hours, moments. As do you. I want to live them all as fully and openly and deliberately as possible.

I go to life itself as naturalist and writer Henry David Thoreau went to the woods.

"I went to the woods," he wrote, "because I wished to live deliberately, to front only the essential facts of life, and see if I could not learn what it had to teach, and not, when I came to die, discover that I had not lived."

When I die, as I surely will, and far sooner than I'd prefer, I want to have lived, to have wrung out the sweet, acidic goodness of the ripe, juicy orange of life, taking in every segment—the fruit, the pulp, the pith, and the zest, devouring it with an abandon that leaves the juice running down my chin.

And though there are many valid approaches to life, I'm convinced that the best way to get the best out of life is through being open to life and the wise lessons it offers, to experience as much as deeply as possible, followed by reflection and contemplation, applying anything gleaned to a continually refined spiritual practice, embracing life more fully as each moment passes.

I believe what Socrates said to be true—that the unexamined life isn't worth living, that my life is my great teacher—just as your life is yours—that the experiences of our lives can be the raw materials for a masterclass on being and becoming, on life and living.

Of course, it doesn't have to be. Like an unread book gathering dust on a bookshelf or a class we're enrolled in but never show up for, our lives can go unexamined, their lessons unlearned, their wisdom ungained.

It's up to us. We get to decide.

WHAT IS YOUR PURPOSE? (Don't get stuck here. This doesn't need to be grand or profound.)

_____

_____

_____

_____

_____

WHAT GIVES you the most meaning, fulfillment, and satisfaction?

---------------------------------------------------------
---------------------------------------------------------
---------------------------------------------------------
---------------------------------------------------------
---------------------------------------------------------
---------------------------------------------------------

# SIX

## School House Rock

LIFE IS LIKE A MONTESSORI SCHOOL. We are allowed to go at our own pace, follow our own path, pursue our own passions, to choose to explore and examine, to learn and grow and evolve and become—or not to. Life's lessons are there, but we have to access them. We have to be active in pursuing our own education.

Life is whispering wisdom to us. Are we listening?

"WISDOM CRIES out in the street;
 she raises her voice in the public squares.
 She calls out at the busiest parts of the noisy streets
 and at the entrance to the gates of the city she utters her words:
 "You naïve ones, how long will you love naiveté?
 And how long will scoffers delight in scoffing

or fools hate knowledge?"


THIS PASSAGE from the Hebrew Bible's book of Proverbs claims that Wisdom cries out, raises her voice in public places, but if she does, she's still challenging to hear—perhaps because of all the other noise.

If we are to hear—and not just hear but perceive—we must listen. And not only listen but actively, mindfully, lovingly, carefully listen.

Life is offering invaluable lessons. Are we learning them? Are we even aware of them? I'm convinced I'm missing most of them.

Writer and theologian Frederick Buechner said it best: "Listen to your life. See it for the fathomless mystery it is. In the boredom and pain of it, no less than in the excitement and gladness: touch, taste, smell your way to the holy and hidden heart of it, because in the last analysis, all moments are key moments, and life itself is grace."

We have to practice engaged listening to hear what our lives are offering us. Be curious. Be courageous. We have to touch, taste, smell, feel, seek, search, look, explore, examine. Life is grace—but we must be willing to be open, reach out and receive that grace. Only when we seek will we find. Only when we investigate the fathomless mystery of our lives will we be transformed by it—by both the mystery and our investigation of it.

Examining our lives—listening to them, learning from them —is something that we can all do. This practice doesn't require a specialized degree or expensive training or even a high IQ. We can start right now, right where we are in life. All that is required is a willingness, a commitment, and a dedicated practice.

Spiritual practices are just that—practices, actions we take, habits we form, a way of being in the world, an approach to life.

Our approach to life largely determines the quality of it. If we are active, open seekers, we will find. If we are careful examiners we will acquire wisdom, we will receive the grace of life, we will experience its mystery.

It's not automatic. It won't just happen. We have to participate in this great learning process. We have to partner with our lives in the way a reader forms a partnership with an author to glean the gifts within the text that connects them.

There are many ways to learn. Some are better than others. Some will work better for us than others. I must determine what works best for me as you must figure out what works best for you. Only I can for me. Only you can for you. Others can help, can offer the gentlest of guidance, but ultimately only we can figure our way through the maze of this most idiosyncratic of educations.

Chinese philosopher Confucius taught: "By three methods we may learn wisdom: First, by reflection, which is noblest; second, by imitation, which is easiest; and third by experience, which is the bitterest."

Learning how we learn best is extremely helpful, but chances are we will learn by all three methods Confucius mentioned—and many others as well.

The life of reflection, which is noblest, is the examined life that is well worth living. It's the act of bringing focused, mindful awareness and evaluation to our days and the ways in which we fill them. By attempting to openly and honestly examine my life, I'm trying to practice a particular form of reflection that will help me better learn life's lessons, enabling me to access and acquire far more wisdom.

But I'm also attempting to learn wisdom through imitation. When I practice compassion, I'm imitating Jesus. When I practice mindful meditation, I'm imitating the Buddha. When I follow the examples of Dr. Martin Luther King, Jr., Frederick Buechner, the poet Thomas Moore, or any number of others who have significant influence over me, I am using the easy, low-hanging fruit of the life lessons of imitation.

But because my ego is too often in control, because I can be defensive and stubborn and resistant, because I can use justification and rationalization like a skillful old pro, I also too often have to learn the hard way. When I refuse to openly, honestly reflect, when I fail to follow the great examples of others, what remains is the bitter elixir of experience—those ways in which life bends and breaks and brings me low. These lessons cut the deepest, leave the most substantial scars, etch themselves in the lines of our faces, and are usually bittersweet gifts we're only grateful for later—when looking back in reflection (because ultimately, it all comes back to this).

And yet, in spite of these three great ways to gain wisdom, I still often fail to learn anything at all. Or I take in only a small part of the lesson the masterful instructor of life is teaching. And when it comes to certain lessons, I do this over and over and over—refusing to learn, refusing to take the remedial class, remaining ignorant and arrogant and unwise.

But if we fail to learn a particular lesson, life has a way of offering it to us again—and again and again. And some lessons take a lifetime to master. I've taken several remedial classes at the University of Life. I'm often slow to learn—defensive, stiff-necked, unteachable—and have to go through a particular class many, many times before beginning to gain the knowledge and wisdom it offers. Not only that, but even when I've already learned certain truths and gained certain insights from a particular lesson, I always learn more and gain new insights when I repeat the class. Each time through the course, I bring more to it and can get more out of it.

But here's the thing. I can learn if I want to.

Wisdom is readily available.

Life is a persistent teacher.

The only way I won't learn is if I'm closed and defensive, militant in my ignorance, convinced I already know the answer, already believing myself to be wise.

Otherwise, I am going to learn, to grow and evolve, to become a wiser, better, more humble and loving version of myself.

That's my heart's desire (which, if true, will show up in the way I live).

So let the listening and examining and reflecting and imitating and experiencing and touching and tasting and feeling my way to the holy hidden heart of life and the wisdom stored there begin. These are things worth amplifying, worth enhancing, worth more productivity, worth doing more of. These make a life worth living and they will lead not to just doing more in life but getting more out of it.

WHAT IS life trying to teach you?

---------------------------------------------------------------
---------------------------------------------------------------
---------------------------------------------------------------
---------------------------------------------------------------
---------------------------------------------------------------
---------------------------------------------------------------

# WHAT IS KEEPING you from learning the lesson?

_____
_____
_____
_____
_____
_____

# SEVEN

**What's your why?**

I believe the most valid reasons to desire to be more productive are related to the quality of our lives, our sense of destiny and purpose, and our desire to enhance our life and the lives of others around us, to utilize the gifts and talents and callings that we've been given to not only make our lives better but to make the world a better place. My desire is to be productive because life is short, sacred, and precious, and because I want to make every moment count.

I have no desire to teach or live a lifestyle of productivity for productivity's sake. So the first and most important question we need to ask is what gives our lives meaning and purpose—what is our identity and what matters most to us? Not only this but how can our purpose and efforts make the world a better place?

What kind of fruit does the tree of our lives produce? Is it good, nutritious, sweet fruit that benefits others? Or is it bitter, rotting fruit that does damage to others? Hitler and his evil hordes were very productive and proficient at mass murder.

Many individuals, organizations, and companies are extremely productive at disseminating misinformation, at making people fearful and then manipulating and controlling them. Others are great at creating and distributing and marketing products that harm people. I would never want to assist in helping any of these individuals, political parties, or corporations become more productive at what they do.

Productivity isn't a practice we can isolate from everything else. What we're productive in and why we're being productive matters. It matters a lot. Hitler's death trains running on time is a horror and atrocity, a perversion of productivity.

How can we be more productive with the things that matter to us, with those things that give our lives purpose and meaning, that relate to our identity and mission? A necessary first question is why do we want to be more productive?

Why do you want to be more productive?

Really ask yourself. It's an important first question. Our whys—the motivations, the intentions behind what we do—are as important as the things we do. Maybe more important. Probably. No, definitely. They're definitely more important.

The German philosopher Friedrich Nietzsche said, "He who has a why to live for can bear almost any how," and Viktor Frankl, the Austrian neurologist, psychiatrist, and Holocaust survivor, testified to the truth of this in what he witnessed in the Holocaust. Even in the very worst of human atrocity and suffering, those who woke up with a why, with a purpose each morning fared far better, even thrived as much as was possible, when compared to those who had no why, no purpose. Knowing your *why* will give you the strength, grace, grit, patience, and persistence to endure the hard work and difficult challenges of the *how* to achieve your dreams.

. . .

**HONESTLY EVALUATE YOUR MOTIVATIONS.** Why do you really do what you do?

---
---
---
---
---

**HOW WILL KNOWING** your why enable you to accomplish more?

---
---
---
---
---

# EIGHT

**Mission**

BEFORE WE EVEN BEGIN TO THINK ABOUT and strategize about being productive, we need to know our mission. What is my mission? Why am I here? What was I created to do? What have I been called to?

Perhaps you've been unable to be as productive as you would like because you're attempting a task outside of your mission.

Knowing your mission, your purpose, your reasons, and your motivations are essential for being productive.

How do you find out your mission?

What are you interested in? What causes something inside you to come alive? What do you do that makes you feel the most fulfilled? What when you do it gives you the greatest sense of meaning? What do you have an affinity for? What are you willing to invest in? What are you willing to spend money on? What are you willing to give thousands and thousands of hours of your life to get proficient at doing?

Answer these questions and you're well on your way to identifying your mission.

But there's another important question.

How can you take what you're interested in and share it with or allow it to be of benefit to others?

For our mission to be valid, sacred, centered in soul instead of ego, it must help others, must in some small way make the world a better place. Our gifts are meant to be given away.

MAKE A LIST OF YOUR INTERESTS:

------------------------------------------------------------
------------------------------------------------------------
------------------------------------------------------------
------------------------------------------------------------
------------------------------------------------------------
------------------------------------------------------------

What are you fascinated by, passionate about? What do you do when you have free time?

------------------------------------------------------------
------------------------------------------------------------
------------------------------------------------------------
------------------------------------------------------------
------------------------------------------------------------
------------------------------------------------------------

DO you have any hidden yearnings? What are they?

_____
_____
_____
_____
_____
_____

WHAT ARE some ways the things you're interested in can help others and make the world a better place?

_____
_____
_____
_____
_____
_____

DO YOU KNOW YOUR MISSION? Can you state it? Do so now. Say it out loud. Write it down. In fact, write it down right here.

## MY MISSION IS:

---------------------------------------------------------------
---------------------------------------------------------------
---------------------------------------------------------------
---------------------------------------------------------------
---------------------------------------------------------------
---------------------------------------------------------------


NOW ASK YOURSELF, do your activities and goals and desires to be productive line up with and relate back to your mission?

If you don't know your mission, your why, your reason for being, I encourage you to spend some time figuring that out before moving on into techniques for being more productive.

# NINE

**Baby, how *you* feel?**

BEFORE WE GET VERY FAR into productivity and having a productive mindset and lifestyle, we need to talk about our wellbeing.

Being productive is dependent on many things, but nothing more so than our mental and physical health.

How do you feel? How are you doing? What is your physical, mental, and emotional state?

We really need to answer these questions honestly and address any issues prior to or at least in conjunction with working on our productivity.

Living our best lives, being our best, most meaningfully productive selves is a challenge when we are in optimum mental and physical condition. But it's damn near impossible when we're not.

I encourage you to do a quick (or slow, if you prefer) assessment of your mental and physical health before moving forward in this book.

How are you sleeping?

How are you eating?

How calm or stressed do you feel?

What are your vitals?

What is your energy level like?

I'm not a doctor, but I can tell you from the jump that if you want to feel better, have a better life, and be more productive, then examine and improve your diet, exercise, and sleep.

I'm sure there's far more you can do, and I'd suggest you talk to your doctor and counselor about what exactly those things are, but sometimes making very small changes to what and how much we're eating and the quantity and quality of exercise and sleep we're getting can make a huge difference.

The point is this: You can never be at optimal productivity levels without being at optimal mental, emotional, and physical health levels.

I have the good fortune of helping care for Autumn, a precious, fun, funny, strong-willed four-year-old little girl, while her mom is at work. It's a privilege and responsibility I take very seriously.

Autumn is like family to me and is an absolute delight. She is energetic, funny, sassy, and has an adorable little personality. At least most of the time.

She often wakes up in a sweet, well-rested, cuddly, kind, caring, slightly sleepy, slightly hoarse-throated state that is the epitome of love and light.

In stark contrast to this, when she gets tired, when she hasn't had enough sleep, when she is in desperate need of the restoration a good nap brings, she is irritable and ill, hypersensitive and overly fragile, whiny, cries, and is even at times rude and mean.

The Jekyll and Hyde divide is the thin, sometimes ragged line between rested and sleep-deprived, hungry and full, overly stimulated and chill.

When Autumn is tired or especially overly tired, this sweet, cute, funny, adorable little girl-child can crash hard, deteriorate quickly, transforming into a hissing, hitting, whiny wild thing.

It occurred to me that we adults are the same way—though we're not always aware of it in ourselves and others to the extent we should be.

There's the well-rested, healthy, balanced best version of ourselves, and then there's the tired, hungry, physically, mentally, and psychologically unwell version of ourselves, the one who is compromised and unkind.

I think if you asked my family and close friends, they would confirm that I'm quite an easygoing chap, a mostly kind and considerate bloke who's mostly loving and caring. However, when I'm not these things, when I'm instead irritable and ill, impatient or short-tempered, it is invariably because I'm tired or stressed or have a chemical imbalance that compromises me to the point of transformation. It's relatively rare and rarely to any great extent, never of the Jekyll and Hyde variety, but it certainly happens on occasion—occasions that no matter how rare they are, are not nearly rare enough to suit me.

To say that you or I act in ways that are unbecoming when we're compromised is in no way saying that being tired or stressed or hungry or a little mentally, emotionally, or spiritually off in any way excuses the resulting bad behavior. These mitigating factors don't excuse, but they do perhaps explain. And maybe the insight gained by perceiving these factors in ourselves and others can lead to greater understanding and eventual grace and compassion—for both ourselves and others.

If I, who am blessed with a good disposition, good health—physically, chemically, mentally, and spiritually—and a good life, can get irritable and short, less kind, less compassionate, less my best self because I'm tired or hungry or sick or stressed, how much more can others whose lives are far more difficult and challenging be influenced, even transformed, by the severe and chronic issues that continuously torture them? And how much more compassion is called for—especially from someone as fortunate as me?

When my children were small, I tried to keep them on a good schedule and in a good routine in order to give them the best chance at being their best selves. Like Autumn and everyone else, they were far better versions of their precious little selves when they were rested and recharged. So much unpleasantness, so many pounds of cure could be avoided by just a bit of planning, just an ounce of prevention. And we'd all do well to parent ourselves that same way. Little Michael is still somewhere inside the grown-ass Michael of today. And sometimes Little Michael needs a nap. And sometimes he needs a sandwich. And sometimes he needs a hug. And sometimes he needs some time out.

And as much as I need to be aware of that, I also need to be aware that the little Blakes and little Joshes and little Brittanys and little Alexes inside the facades of their current grown-ass incarnations may need a hell of a lot more than a nap and a sandwich, which is why they act out in ways that are much more hurtful and harmful to themselves and others than some slight irritability or minor self-centeredness. And as frightening a thought as it is, like me, they may be doing the best they can. And perhaps, like me, with some love and understanding—and in some cases a good treatment program or a well-trained professional counselor—they'll be even better and do even better. They just need a bit of care, a bit of parenting, a modicum of understanding. How much less of the man I think

I am—or at least aspire to be—would I be if I can't give them that?

I think this is why the philosopher Plato said, "Be kind, for everyone you meet is fighting a harder battle."

How many times have I judged someone's attitude, actions, words, and behaviors without considering the battle they're fighting? How often have I, self-centeredly, narcissistically projected onto someone how good I was feeling and judged them because their words and actions weren't commensurate with feeling so well, which, of course, they probably weren't?

I believe Jesus said "judge not" because we don't know shit about what's really going on in and with anyone else and so are always making our ruling on the most partial circumstantial evidence.

Like a fever or a rash or swelling, perhaps many or even most of the bad behaviors we see in ourselves and others are symptoms that indicate an infection in our mind, a sickness in our soul—or even something as straightforward and obvious as fatigue or hunger or a hormonal imbalance.

Be kind—to yourself and others and to the little ones still inside. Get some sleep. Eat a sandwich. Meditate. Declutter. Destress. Detox. And help others do the same. And when you don't—and when they don't—give lots and lots of grace. I mean go all medieval with that shit—spread it around with liberal abandon, make grace rain like singles at a strip club on a busy Saturday night during bike week. Because we all need it—and who knows, maybe she really is a single mom putting herself through college. But even if that's as false as our own most deceptive facades, there's a reason for it—probably a glitter bottle full of them.

Give yourself grace. And give it to others. And remember, grace is needed most when we're at our least. It's the absolute best for our absolute worst.

I have more to say—much more. I haven't even started to torture the "grace as singles in a strip club" metaphor yet, but Little Michael is hungry and sleepy, so I'm going to stop here for now and go make myself a sandwich and take a nap—two things I highly recommend you do before attempting to be productive.

Give yourself grace. Get some rest and sleep. Eat well. Be mindful, and practice peace not perfection. All of these will help you feel your best to be your best, most productive self, and if they don't, see your doctor.

HOW CAN you be healthier beginning today?

------------------------------------------------------------
------------------------------------------------------------
------------------------------------------------------------
------------------------------------------------------------
------------------------------------------------------------
------------------------------------------------------------

WHAT ARE some small changes to your diet, exercise regimen, and sleep routines that you can make today that will have a big impact on the quality of your life and your productivity?

------------------------------------------------------------
------------------------------------------------------------
------------------------------------------------------------
------------------------------------------------------------
------------------------------------------------------------
------------------------------------------------------------

WHAT ARE YOU WAITING FOR?

# TEN

## The Ticking Clock

THE TICKS of the clock are relentless.

This is part of what motivates me to be productive, to get the most out of this life that I can. As far as any of us know, this is the only one we get, and what we do with it is what matters most.

Clocks never slow down, but they never speed up either. Each of us is given the same twenty-four hours every single day and we get to choose what we do with them. I want to make the most of my life. Life itself is a gift and what I do with it is my response to that gift and determines the way in which I share that gift with the world. I want the gift of my existence to enhance the lives of others, to be of benefit to them. This is why I want to be more productive in the areas that matter most—not for accomplishment's sake, not for recognition, applause, or accolades, but for meaning and fulfillment.

We try to insulate ourselves from the loud, reverberating

*tick, tick, tick, tick, tick* of the clocks of our lives, but that's a huge mistake. Interestingly, clocks themselves used to remind us with inscribed mottos like *ultima forsan,* "perhaps the last" or *vulnerant omnes, ultima necat,* "they all wound, and the last kills."

Even as you read this, the sands in the hourglass of your life are running out.

I don't have infinite time or resources. I must make choices.

I want to live my best life possible, to get the most out of every moment, to be fully awake and alive and maximize and enjoy every second.

Every Tuesday is trash day at our house. I gather it, take it to the big green outside garbage can, and then roll that can to the street. And every Tuesday I think, *I just did this. How can it be trash day again? Is my life really passing by this quickly?* As I do, I reflect on all the life I have packed in during the previous week, which is usually a shit ton, and yet I feel forlorn, a deep sense of sadness at just how fast the sands of my hourglass are bleeding out. I don't want my life to be measured from trash day to trash day, and I don't want to not have done what matters most when the next trash day rolls around.

Why be productive? Because time is short and precious. It's all we have and yet we're always running out of it.

The greatest tragedy possible is to come to the end of our lives—whenever that may be—and realize we've not lived.

Because of the brevity of life, we must prioritize what matters most and do that first and foremost every day, every moment. Throughout our lives we are continuously being confronted with choices. At every moment, two roads diverge in the yellow woods of our lives. And we must choose which one to take. The one to take is the one that most aligns with who we are, our mission, our purpose, our goals, with the kind of person we want to be, the kind of life we want to have.

. . .

WHAT DO you think your *ultima forsan, your last act,* will be? What do you want it to be?

---

HOW CAN you live more deliberately, front the essentials of life, and ensure that you truly live before you die?

---

# ELEVEN

**What's on your mind?**

THIS FIRST SECTION ON MOTIVATION, purpose, calling, and mindset is the most important of the book.

Our mindsets are far more important than any strategy or plan or program to be productive. That's why I'm starting with it, why I'm stressing it. How we think about our lives, what motivates us, and what our mentalities are matter more than anything else.

If we have the right mindset, we'll be productive—we'll do the most and get the most out of our lives. As Chinese philosopher Lao Tzu teaches:

"WATCH YOUR THOUGHTS; They become words;
 Watch your words; They become actions;
 Watch your actions; They become habits;
 Watch your habits; They become your character;

Watch your character; It becomes your destiny."


HOW DO you think about your life? The gifts, talents, and opportunities you've been given? What is your purpose? What gives you meaning and fulfillment? Prioritize these things. This is the *how* of productivity, the *why*, the motivation, the foundation.

Are you trying to make yourself be more productive for productivity's sake? No wonder you find it so difficult, frustrating, and inconsistent.

What I'm talking about here—what will make you the most productive you can be, the best version of yourself you can achieve—is productivity with a purpose. What is your purpose? What are your goals? What were you created to do? You will only have your best life, you will only be your most productive, when your purpose and productivity, your mission and your actions all align.

It doesn't seem to be the case so much anymore, but it used to be that our vehicles would get knocked out of alignment. They'd hit a deep pothole or take some hard bounces over a railroad track and start pulling in one direction or the other instead of staying straight in their given lane. I don't notice this as much on vehicles these days, but it seems as if every shopping cart I get at the grocery store suffers from this same issue.

If our mission, purpose, goals, motivations, the meaning of our lives and our actions aren't aligned, then the steering wheel is going to constantly pull in another direction. When we have to fight against the pull of misalignment, we get a lot less done. And it's exhausting.

If you are continually exhausted, if you are frustrated because you're not getting more done, it may very well be it's because what you're attempting to do doesn't line up with what you're called to do, what you were created to do—it is out of alignment with where your interests, gifts, talents, and callings lie.

Managing our minds is the single most important thing we can do in life. It's foundational to everything else. Examine your thoughts. Attempt to look at them critically and objectively. You are not your thoughts. You are the thinker, the observer.

Experts say we have between fifty thousand and seventy thousand thoughts a day. That's an extraordinary amount, but all we need to concern ourselves with are the thoughts that stick, that don't just float through our minds. These are the ones that trigger an emotion, bring up some unresolved issue or pain, which is why they're not just floating on through. We cling to them, identify with them, create our stories around them, nurse the wound of them, and waste so much of our lives.

Through mindfulness and meditation we can practice letting go. We can create the space we need between the thought and the thinker. But for those thoughts that are triggering you, spend some time examining, exploring, and healing so you can release instead of cling to them, so you can be truly free to manage your mind and do more of what truly matters in this all-too-brief life.

Create a thought journal. Over the course of at least a week, write down what you are thinking.

WRITE down some of your recent thoughts:

_____
_____
_____
_____

---
---

CREATE separation between you as the thinker and the thoughts that float through your mind. Sing your thoughts. Say them with a different accent.

Ask these questions of every thought you have: Is it true? Can you really know it's true? Is it important? Does it really matter? Is it useful? Does having this thought benefit you in any way? Is this thought helping me live a better life?

TAKE your most troubling experiences and the thoughts that accompany them, write them out and explore and examine them:

1. An event or thought occurs. What is it?

---
---
---
---
---
---

2. I tell myself something about it. What do I tell myself?

---
---

3. I feel certain emotions because of what I've told myself. What do I feel?

ASK YOURSELF: Are these thoughts true? Can you really know they are true? Why do they trigger you, make you feel something? Where are you getting stuck? How can you let go? Why do you choose to suffer instead of releasing the thought and the emotion that it triggers? What is the payoff? What would your life be without these thoughts and feelings? How much more time and energy would you have to be productive, to do what matters most to you?

# TWELVE

**You Are What You Practice**

PRACTICE IS the actual application or use of an idea, belief, or method, as opposed to theories relating to it. It's about what we actually do, not just what we think or believe.

We become what we practice.

As philosopher Aristotle noted, "We are what we repeatedly do. Excellence is not an event—it is a habit."

The more we practice productivity, the better we get at it. If we are to be our best selves and have our most productive lives, then productivity as a practice must become a lifestyle. It must become what we do, who we are, not just something we attempt on the odd occasion.

How do we close the gap between the person we are and the person we want to be? Through practice. By becoming. By making the right choice each moment. By taking the next right action. Because choice leads to choice, and what we do in this moment is what matters most.

As Robert Frost reminds us, *The Road Not Taken* is as important as the one taken.


"TWO ROADS DIVERGED in a yellow wood,
    And sorry I could not travel both
    And be one traveler, long I stood
    And looked down one as far as I could
    To where it bent in the undergrowth;


AND BOTH THAT morning equally lay
    In leaves no step had trodden black.
    Oh, I kept the first for another day!
    Yet knowing how way leads on to way,
    I doubted if I should ever come back."


EXAMINE the moments of your life. Every moment matters. The choices we make in each moment, no matter how small they seem at the time, actually determine the course and quality of our lives.

Every choice we make matters. Not only for their own sake, but for what they lead to and what they lead away from.

*Yet knowing how way leads on to way,*
*I doubted if I should ever come back.*

Way leads on to way. Every choice we make takes us in a certain direction and simultaneously away from other directions. We can never return to this present moment again. It's already gone. And now so is another. And another. We can never step into the same river twice. Time and tide move on.

Way leads on to way, and we can never return. Choose wisely. "Everything that exists in your life, does so because of two things; something you did or something you didn't do," theoretical physicist Albert Einstein said.

Every choice we make either enhances our lives, makes us better, wiser, more compassionate, healthier, happier, of more benefit to others, or it doesn't.

We are what we practice. We are what we choose. We become what we love, what we do.

I'm good at what I've practiced consistently for decades. I'm not good at everything else.

Talent is overrated. Practice is all.

If you worry and fret and live in fear, you become a master at that.

If you practice trust and love and compassion and peace, you become a master at that.

You and I are making choices right now that determine who we are, who we become, that actually create the quality of our lives.

Who we are isn't who we think we are, isn't who we want to be, isn't who we believe we are. It's what we practice. I am what I practice. You are what you practice.

"Practice makes perfect" is only true if we use the definition of perfect that means complete—like sweet, juicy ripened fruit.

A tree is known by its fruit—by the fruit it *produces*. The tree of your life is producing fruit. Taste it. Is it good or bad? Sweet or bitter? Want to change anything or everything about it? Change your choices.

Change your choices. Change your life. Change your practices. Change what you produce.

Examine your life closely and carefully. What are your patterns? What are you doing habitually? Make a list.

. . .

**LOOKING AT MY LIFE,** I find that I consistently practice:

---------------------------------------------------------
---------------------------------------------------------
---------------------------------------------------------
---------------------------------------------------------
---------------------------------------------------------
---------------------------------------------------------

**THE THINGS** I want to be practicing instead are:

---------------------------------------------------------
---------------------------------------------------------
---------------------------------------------------------
---------------------------------------------------------
---------------------------------------------------------
---------------------------------------------------------

**KEEP READING.** Throughout the course of this book we will examine how to change our mindsets and our practices in order to get more done of what matters most.

# THIRTEEN

## What Matters Most

PRODUCTIVITY IS NOT an end unto itself.

I'm not trying to be more productive in general but in particular. And I hope you are too.

I have no desire to be more productive in areas that are outside of my purpose, my mission, my calling.

I want to be more productive in doing the things that matter most. And I want the same for you.

What are your priorities? What are the most meaningful, valuable, purposeful priorities in your life? If you're not sure, take some time to identify them first.

For me, in this moment, my priorities are my family, friends, and loved ones, my health and wholeness, my writing, my music, my teaching/counseling. These are the areas I want to be the most productive in. What are yours?

Once we identify our purpose, our mission, our why, we can devote our time, attention, and resources to them.

Part of the reason we're not nearly as productive as we want to be is that we're not putting first things first—we've not identified what matters most and we're not living with an acute awareness of where we're spending our time, attention, focus, energy, money, etc.

We've got to be honest with ourselves about what we really care about. Too often we claim the priorities of others, we say what we think we're supposed to say, what our culture or family or religion tells us are the right things to say. Spend some time and focus on what your actual priorities are, make adjustments as necessary and then allocate the short time and limited resources you have to being productive in these areas.

I don't just say that my family and loved ones are a priority to me, I live it. I spend a huge part of my time, attention, energy, finances, and other resources on my closest intimates. And I've arranged my life (my priorities and productivity) to ensure that I can do this consistently.

From the moment my children were born, I arranged my schedule to maximize my time with them. I was and still am fully present in their lives. When writing a novel, I don't lock myself away somewhere, only to emerge months or years later when it's complete. When I wrote my first novel from 1994 until 1997, my daughter was between four and seven and my son was between zero and three. I wrote it with them on my knee, with constant interruptions, stops and starts, and I've written each subsequent book that same way.

Since I began writing in the summer of 1994, I've written nearly every day. Since I started playing guitar and singing in the fall of 2018, I've practiced nearly every single day. I have taught and counseled and attempted to inspire others since I was a teenager, and I've spent nearly every day since then practicing and doing it. And I've done all these things in and around and with my loved ones—being available to them and as present in their lives as possible. These are some of my main and most important priorities and the areas where I am the most productive. These are also the areas where I'm continually tweaking my productivity to be even more efficient and effective. I'm not attempting to be more productive in many other areas because they don't matter—or don't matter nearly as much as these do.

Don't be productive in general. Be productive in particular. Do what matters most and do it first.

Look at how you spend your "free" time and how you spend your "disposable" income. Whether you like it or not, these are your priorities. If they aren't aligned with your calling, mission, and purpose, change them. Make edits in the manuscript of your life. Make alterations in the garment of your existence. The soil of your soul only has a limited amount of nutrients. Snatch out the weeds of wasted time and energy and resources and reallocate them to the flowers and fruit trees of your life, to that which matters most.

MAKE a list of what matters most to you. Write down only the few things that truly matter most to you—your priorities:

----------------------------------------------------------------
----------------------------------------------------------------
----------------------------------------------------------------
----------------------------------------------------------------
----------------------------------------------------------------
----------------------------------------------------------------

ARE you truly giving priority to these things? How could you close the gap between what you say matters most and what you're actually spending your limited time and resources on?

---------------------------------------------------------------
---------------------------------------------------------------
---------------------------------------------------------------
---------------------------------------------------------------
---------------------------------------------------------------
---------------------------------------------------------------

# FOURTEEN

**Ask Yourself . . .**

CAN you identify what matters most to you?
   Do you have a sense of purpose?
   Do you know your mission?
   Can you state your mission in a few sentences?
   Do your goals match your mission?
   How are you spending your "free" time?
   What are you spending your "disposable" income on?
   Are there ways in which what you're doing with your time and resources doesn't align with your purpose, mission, goals?
   Are you as productive in the areas that matter most as you'd like to be? If not, can you identify why not?
   Make a list of the blackholes and rabbit holes in your life that kill your productivity, that drain your energy, that distract you from what matters most.

# PART TWO
# TIPS, TRICKS, HACKS, AND HABITS

# FIFTEEN

**Prioritize, Organize, Listerize**

ONCE WE HAVE our minds right, we are ready to become more productive. There are many places we could start, but I think a good place is with a bit of organization. Being productive is not just about what we produce but what we choose not to produce. We cannot do everything, and being productive is about choosing the things we can do and will do as well as choosing the things we can't do or won't do.

Don't wait. Start where you are. Do something. Make a change.

A better life is not awaiting you across some green field, in a different city, on a different day. It's available this very moment.

Don't wait.

Be honest about where you are. You have to start from there. Don't pretend to be on a rung of the ladder that you're not on. Don't attempt to begin from a place you're not in.

Take small strides if you have to. But begin. Make a step, even if a single one, in the right direction.

The concept of repentance is as simple and complex as doing an about-face. We realize we're headed in the wrong direction and we turn around. Simple. Perhaps not easy, but it's not a difficult or abstract concept. It's easy to grasp. In whatever ways and in whatever areas you realize you're headed in the wrong direction, do an about-face. Take a step in the right direction.

# SIXTEEN

**Prioritize**

A critical first step in productivity is prioritizing what we want to accomplish. Many of us aren't as productive as we could be, as we would like to be, not because we do too little, but because we try to do too much. We're wasting time doing the wrong things or doing a little of a lot of different things and not actually finishing much of anything. Remember, we can't do everything. Being productive is as much about what we choose not to do as it is what we choose to do. Way leads on to way. Every choice matters. What is most important? Do those things—and do them first!

For a while now there have been a lot of books, blogs, articles, and Ted Talks about not giving a fuck, but many people seem to miss the point of these various presentations. The key to a happy, productive, meaningful, and fulfilling life is not in not giving a fuck about anything. It's in knowing what to give a fuck about. You and I only have so many fucks to give, so we have to use our fucks carefully and judiciously.

One of the keys to having our best lives is to prioritize that which matters most to us and focus our time, energy, attention, and resources there, while simultaneously letting go of everything else.

The truth is we can't do everything. We have a finite amount of time, energy, interest, ability, etc. The key to a productive life, to our best lives possible, is figuring out what matters most and doing as much of those things as possible. Everything doesn't matter equally. There are things that are far, far more important than others. Until we understand this, we're going to waste much of our limited time and resources on things that are ultimately empty and unfulfilling and keep us away from doing the things that matter most.

At this very moment you and I have priorities that we are living by, but it's entirely possible that those priorities don't match the ones in our heads. We believe certain things are important to us, and maybe they really are, but if you look at how we live, at what we're actually doing with our lives—our time, money, resources, energy, and attention—we're not living as though they are our priorities at all.

You and I need to, as quickly as possible, close the gap between what we say matters most to us and what we're actually doing with our lives. This as much as anything else will change our lives, will cause us to be more productive, fruitful, and fulfilled.

When we're not as productive as we want to be, it may be that we're simply not doing enough, but it's more likely that we're doing too much of the wrong things. Any time and energy you and I spend on things that don't matter or matter less than other things takes time and energy away from what really does matter to us.

We've got to have priorities and they have to be the right priorities. We've got to prioritize the work, the doing of the thing, not the desire, not the thinking or talking about it.

It's not enough to want to do something. It's not enough to think about it or read about it or study it. We must prioritize the *doing* of it.

Some twenty-seven years ago, I wanted to become a novelist. What if I hadn't done anything with that desire? Or what if I had done only certain things with it—thought about it, read about it, took some classes, attended some workshops? Admired others who were doing it?

If that's all I had done, my life would be very different today. In the nearly three decades that have passed, I've written some forty books. But what if I hadn't? What if today, over a quarter of a century later, I was still just nursing the desire?

Our priorities must be to actually do what we're wanting to.

I am willing to bet you that there were many people in the world twenty-seven years ago when I became a novelist who, like me, wanted to be a novelist, but who have yet to produce a novel. The difference is in the doing—in prioritizing our to-dos so that we get shit to-done.

Do you know what they call a writer who doesn't give up? An author!

What if three years ago when I wanted to play the guitar, I had bought some books about it or even gone as far as purchasing a guitar? I wouldn't be playing today. Instead of just wanting to play the guitar, I prioritized my time, energy, and effort to actually start playing, and by maintaining that priority every single day—even when my fingers hurt, even when I was tired, even when I felt like my progress was too slow—I have seen dramatic improvement.

I wish you could ask your future self what you would like your current self to be doing, and in a way you can.

Three or thirty years from now you'll want to have actually done certain things. Now is the time to do them. Make a start. Set a goal, then prioritize your days starting today. That's the only way to get where you want to go, and your future you will thank you.

You and I have an extremely limited amount of time, energy, attention, resources. Wasting them on things that don't matter is nothing short of wasting our lives.

Figure out your priorities. Allocate your resources there—mental, spiritual, emotional, physical, financial. You will become happier, more productive, and have a far, far more meaningful life.

MAKE A LIST OF YOUR PRIORITIES:

_____
_____
_____
_____
_____
_____

EXAMINE YOUR LIFE. Take a look at what you're doing with your time, energy, attention, and resources. Make a list of the things that don't matter or don't matter much that are consuming too much of your time and energy:

_____
_____
_____
_____
_____
_____

WANT TO CHANGE YOUR LIFE? Want to become instantly more productive? Stop spending so much of your time, energy, and resources on the items on your second list and divert them to the items on your first list.

Your very best life is awaiting you—figure out what actually matters most to you and prioritize those things.

# SEVENTEEN

**Organize**

YOU DO NOT HAVE to have a certain organizational system in order to optimize your productivity. But you do have to be organized. It's up to you to figure out the best way to organize your workspace, workflow, and ultimately your work—but figure it out you must in order to be as productive as possible. The good news is you only have to figure out what works best for you.

Experts tell us that external clutter clutters the mind. Perhaps you are convinced you create better in chaos and clutter. Perhaps you do. Who am I to say that you don't? But I challenge you to at least give a decluttered, organized workspace and workflow a try. If you don't produce more while having more peace of mind, you can always return to what worked for you before.

When I first started writing novels, I wanted someone to tell me how to do it. I took classes, attended workshops, read books, and talked to other authors. And what I discovered during this process was that I had to figure out how *I* write a novel—and, in fact, I have to do that every time I write a new novel. Learning how to do something such as novel writing or whatever it is you're attempting to do is an idiosyncratic endeavor, and figuring out how *you* do it is essential to actually being able to do it—and a huge part of this is how you organize your work environment, workflow, and your work itself.

You do not have to have a dedicated space to do your work, but it really helps. You do not have to do your work at the same time every day, but it really helps. If you're able to create a dedicated sacred space all your own, no matter how small it may be, and if you're able to organize it so that it works for you so that it enables you to do your work, you will be far more productive and be so consistently than if you take a haphazard unorganized approach. Look at your desktop, the one on your computer as well as your actual desktop workspace. Is it cluttered? Is it neat? Can you find what you need quickly in order to do your work efficiently? If not, spending some time getting organized will be time well spent in the pursuit of greater productivity.

For my entire adult life I've had a dedicated creative work space. It was a walk-in closet in my first apartment. It was an upstairs room at a neighbor's house when my young family lived in a small two-bedroom rental. For the past twenty-five plus years, it has been a large library/study/scriptorium/sanctuary. It is filled with tens of thousands of books, art, photography, an altar, meaningful mementos, pictures of my children and loved ones, candles, incense, special lighting, guitars, the notebooks and journals and computers I need to do my work. I use a laptop on a special stand in my writing chair to write fiction. I use a desktop on my desk to do everything else—email, Amazon, YouTube meditations, Ted Talks, social media, watching porn, shopping for guitars, audio and video editing, etc. It's hard to imagine a space more sacred to me, more conducive to my creativity and spirituality, yet I continually try to improve on it, iterate and organize it in ways that make me even more productive.

This is what works for me. Find what works for you.

My partner used to work in an open room right next to the kitchen and living room. In it she achieved a high level of productivity. However, when we created a dedicated space for her upstairs away from the noise and traffic and interruptions of the kitchen and living room, her productivity and mental health increased exponentially.

Remember, talent isn't what determines success. Systems do. Practices do. Hard work does. Creating a work environment and workflow that works for you is foundational to everything else you do and will have an enormous impact on what and how much you produce.

Either your workspace and workflow is optimal for your work (and sanity) or it's not. If it's not, change it. If it is, improve it even more. Your investments here will yield incredible results in the quality and quantity of your life and work.

# EIGHTEEN

**Listerize**

MAKING a realistic list of what we want to accomplish in a given day is a vital component in increasing our productivity.

*Verba volant. Scripta manent.* These words tattooed on my right biceps are meant to remind me that "spoken words fly away, written words remain." Perhaps unsurprising words for a writer to have etched into his skin, but they are critical for anyone who wants to get things done and keep life from fruitlessly ebbing away.

Relying upon our memory is dangerous. Working from a list reminds us of what we want to accomplish and keeps us on task as we refer back to it and check in with it.

Don't just make a list. Make a prioritized list.

Create a calendar. Block out time for your tasks—but do so according to your priorities.

We most often do our best work first, earliest, so prioritize your most important tasks so you can do them when you are at your best. In writing, we call these morning pages. And morning pages, when we have just woken up and our minds are fresh and refreshed and we're still dreamily connected to our subconscious, are the very best and most creatively productive.

As someone who has earned his daily bread from writing for over two decades, my productivity and my income are directly related. I make a living from my art and craft and must maintain a certain consistent productivity to do so. There's a Bible verse that says something like *If you don't work, you don't eat.* For me, if I don't write, I don't eat.

I have found over the years that working from a list is an extremely effective and efficient way to maintain consistency in my productivity.

Every morning I make a list for that day.

I work from my daily lists and find great satisfaction in checking off the items I accomplish.

Over decades of working from lists, I don't think there's ever been a single day that I completely finished my list and was able to check off everything on it. That's why it's so important to prioritize the list and do what matters most first. Each morning when I'm making that day's list, I move the items that I didn't complete the previous day onto it.

In addition to working from a daily list, I think it's important to have a list of long-term goals, the things that can't be accomplished in a single day. It's too easy to forget about these things, too easy to lose sight of the forest of our mission by focusing too intently on the single trees of our daily lists.

Having a mission statement helps. Referring to it often reminds us of where our energy and effort need to be.

I write my daily to-do lists in my journal and work through them and refer back to them throughout each day. But I also have lists of larger long-term goals. In fact, they are framed and hanging in various places in my house. I have three hanging next to my desk as I write this.

These long-term goals lists are made up of the things that matter most, and my daily lists should be informed by them. The items on my daily to-do list should relate directly back to my yearly and lifetime goals lists.

I'm a Lister—by birth and by practice. This is what works for me. But I think it can work for everyone, and I highly recommend you give it a try.

It's a good, wise practice to write down what matters most. It's too easy to forget what we don't write down, too easy to not remember let alone accomplish those things we don't write down, don't keep in front of us.

Make a list. Check it twice. Be mindful of how you're spending your life.

WHAT ARE YOUR LIFETIME GOALS? Make a list of them (refer back to the obituary you wrote):

------------------------------------------------
------------------------------------------------
------------------------------------------------
------------------------------------------------
------------------------------------------------
------------------------------------------------

MAKE a list of what you want to accomplish today:

_____
_____
_____
_____
_____
_____

DOES what you want to accomplish today relate to and support what you want to accomplish over your lifetime? How? Are there any ways it doesn't? How can you edit and iterate your daily list to ensure that you are working toward your lifetime goals?

# NINETEEN

**Rest**

REST AND RELAXATION are not only absolute essentials for being productive but can be productive activities in and of themselves.

As a young person, I hated having to sleep. I resented it. I fought against it. To this day I wish I didn't have to sleep, but I now see just how critically important it is to health, creativity, productivity, to having my best life possible.

It would be foolish, shortsighted, and ultimately catastrophic in our attempts to be more productive to attempt to excise rest, relaxation, and recreation from our lives.

A productive life is a balanced life. And again, our goal is not machine-like production in a single area, but our best lives lived in health and harmony, lives that are rich and full, fun and meaningful.

Add rest and relaxation to your list, to your goals and priorities—not just sleep, but rest, entertainment, downtime, doing nothing or not much of anything. Unproductivity is essential to productivity.

All of the great wisdom traditions of the world have within them the concept of rest that is more than rest, that is sacred. In Judaism it's the Sabbath, a set-aside seventh day to rest, reflect, recharge. That same concept is also extended to years and the cycles of borrowing and lending and the land's use for planting and harvesting.

Rest. Relax. Have fun. Enjoy your life. And don't feel guilty for doing so. Our best lives prioritize rest, relaxation, fun, and entertainment, not just single-minded focus on producing more work.

# TWENTY

**The Space Between**

THE SPACE between things matters nearly as much as the things themselves.

The silence between musical notes, the white space between paragraphs in prose and poetry, and the emptiness in a bowl are not just vital but actually give definition to everything else.

From the Taoist philosophical, the *Tao Te Ching*:

"HOLLOWED OUT,
 clay makes a pot.
 Where the pot's not
 is where it's useful."

. . .

YOU CAN'T HAVE a bowl without an empty space, without the space between.

Maintaining a certain type of open emptiness is essential for growth, evolution, becoming. We're often too full to increase either our productivity or the quality of our lives.

Less is often more. Do less in order to do more.

Be empty in order to have room for input, inspiration, and increased spirituality.

Honor the emptiness, the spaces—particularly those in between activities we deem important.

Emptiness can be the open space we need most to be who we want to be, to do what we want to do, but it can also be just wasted space, an empty unused room with some random mismatched furniture and junk.

One of the most crucial steps you and I can take to increase our productivity is to decrease the time, space, and energy between the activities that matter most. This is especially true when those empty spaces are blackholes of lost time and energy.

Too much of our time, of our very lives, is wasted by meandering aimlessly between activities that truly matter to us and align with our mission and purpose.

One of the ways that I have increased my productivity over the years is not wasting time between the things that I do.

I'm not saying we should rush from activity to activity in some sort of ADHD fever, just that we evaluate how we're spending our time in between the things that matter most to us. If we're spending them in positive, productive emptiness, then we should keep it up, but if we're merely wasting time, we should consider compressing the time and space between.

The sooner you and I compress the wasted time and space between the activities and pursuits that matter most to us, the sooner we will expand and extend the quality and quantity of our lives.

We only have so much bandwidth, so much energy, so much strength, so much interest, so much ability, and how we allocate those resources determines not only our productivity but the actual depth and length of our lives.

When I complete one of the items on my to-do list, I can move to the next one or I can waste a lot of time trying to decide what I'm going to do next, surfing the Internet, looking at Facebook, watching YouTube, or just stewing in my indecision.

I'm considered a prolific novelist, but I know of writers who put my output to shame. They use a number of techniques and strategies to achieve their staggering production, such as dictation. They are able to dictate far more words in an hour than they can type. I don't employ this strategy because I like the tactile process of writing, typing, of my fingers dancing across the keyboard, but I know it works.

Another strategy prolific novelists employ is preparing what we're going to write before we sit down to write it.

If I spend time preparing what I'm going to write, then when I sit down at the keyboard I don't waste a lot of time wondering what I'm going to write or trying to come up with something to write. I simply write.

This is a way of managing and maximizing time. This form of preparation helps compress time between activities and leads to greater productivity. And we can employ this in every aspect of our lives.

We all know that the shortest route between two points is the most direct. There are many times in life where we don't want to take the direct route. The scenic route is far more soul-nourishing, relaxing, and appealing, which is a wonderful type of productivity in and of itself. But when there is no scenic route, when our goal is to do an activity followed by another activity, then decreasing the distance between those two points provides more time at each point, for each activity.

If you and I finish an activity and sit around and spend time congratulating ourselves and feeling good about what we've done, all we're doing is draining time from a future activity—and ultimately we get less done. We will not only have less time for the activities that matter most to us, but we'll also have less energy, attention, and focus.

If you want to share a great meal with your loved ones, and your goal is to have nourishment for the body as well as the soul —a loving table of fellowship and companionship, a warm sense of connection while sharing a great meal—you can go about facilitating this in many different ways.

You may want to prepare the meal and serve it in addition to hosting, sitting, and visiting with your loved ones. If this is the case, you may find it beneficial and productive and soul-building to take a leisurely drive to the grocery store and then wander up and down the aisles in search of inspiration for just the right ingredients for the meal you want to create. You may then wander back home in the same leisurely manner then spend your time in the kitchen doing many other things in addition to cooking and preparing the meal. When your guests arrive, the meal may not be ready and that may be absolutely okay with everyone and you may visit and have cocktails while finishing up the meal you're creating. And this may be the best, most fulfilling approach you could take.

And yet . . .

It may be that you don't enjoy or benefit from every element of driving and shopping and cooking and hosting and feasting equally. And it may be that you have other things you want to accomplish during this particular day. It may be that you find it more productive and less wasteful not to meander on the way to the store or in it once you get there. It may be that deciding ahead of time what you're going to prepare and preparing a shopping list of the ingredients you need will cause you to have a better experience at the store and cause you to be able to get in and out more quickly to give you more time for the meal preparation, more time to spend with your guests, more energy to spend on them and other things.

EITHER APPROACH IS NOT ONLY valid but can be productive in its own way—may, in fact, be exactly what our hearts and souls and lives in bodies and minds need. You have to figure out what your priorities are and what you want out of your life and out of your experiences in general and at any given moment in particular, and only you can do that for you. For me, shopping for a meal, preparing it, and sharing it with my loved ones wouldn't be the only things I'd want to accomplish that day. I'd want to get up and write my morning pages before I did anything else. I would want to spend time with friends and family. I would want to get some exercise in. I'd want to meditate, journal, reflect. I'd want to play some basketball, play some guitar and sing. I'd want to read, to have sex, and do many other activities that are vitally important to me, that make my life fulfilling and rewarding—are what matter most to me.

I would want to compress the time of travel to and from the store. I would want to compress the time spent shopping. I would want to work from a list and not get distracted by all the other items in the store. I don't find wandering around a grocery store particularly productive for me, so I would attempt to shorten that aspect of this process.

In fact, it may be that instead of shopping for and creating a meal, I would instead take my loved ones out to eat and so maximize our time together at the table and also give me the opportunity to accomplish other things before and after the shared meal experience. This may not be true for you. Only you can determine what matters most to you. Only you can implement those things in your life.

I encourage you to figure out what matters most to you and to place your time, energy, attention, and focus on them. And one of the ways you may actually have more time, energy, attention, and focus is by compressing the time between activities that are draining you, are robbing you, are keeping you from what matters most.

One of the great pleasures in my life is basketball. I not only enjoy watching basketball, but I enjoy playing it—and do so three or four times a week.

I started playing in childhood and have played consistently throughout my entire life.

In the past few years, I have been playing more pick-up games than anything else. This is where we all just show up at the gym and pick teams from who shows up on a given night.

One of the things I find most frustrating when I play pick-up is the time wasted between games. We could fit far more games in and have more time to invest in other things if we spent less time in wasted waiting between games.

You and I have wasted time in our lives, energy leaks that are robbing us from what we really want to be doing more of. Our best, most productive and meaningful lives will be aided by editing those parts out.

Put some smoke in the lines of your life. When a plumber wants to test for leaks, for broken pipes, she will shoot smoke into the pipes and then observe where it leaks out. Closely examine your life. Keep a journal, a calendar, an account of where your time, energy, and resources are going. Smoke out the leaks that are weakening the flow of your life and keeping you from achieving what matters most, Robbing you of the life you want.

# TWENTY-ONE

**Focus**

If you examine anyone who has mastered what they do, you'll find that not only have they spent countless hours practicing and perfecting their work, but that they have a deep capacity for deep focus, the ability to get lost in what they do.

The greatest actors are those who are so focused that they become the character they're playing, they are fully present in the scene as that character and only respond as that character. That's why they say all great acting is actually *reacting*.

This phenomenon is often described as getting into *the zone* in sports. It's when world-class athletes play unconsciously—not thinking about the next play or their next move, just making it, seemingly part of an unseen ballet that has been choreographed to perfection.

This type of deep-focus performance, this kind of living embodiment of a profound poem, is the result of countless hours of deep-concentration practice in perfecting art and craft.

For you and me to be our most productive, to produce our best work, is going to require a deep-focus doing and redoing and doing again—countless hours of concentration in pursuit of perfection.

All the experts agree: Talent is overrated—and nearly always the least important part of any equation involving excellence.

What then is required to become excellent, productive, proficient? Practice. But not just any practice. Deep-focus, exhausting practice done daily with critique and feedback for years on end—some ten years or ten thousand hours for starters.

If you and I want to be good at something, we must invest heavily, work our asses off, find a mentor who is already a master and welcome his or her feedback. And never stop practicing, learning, growing, evolving in our pursuit of excellence.

The sad and painful truth is that we are often not very good at something because we've been unwilling to do the work, unwilling to invest the time, unwilling to exhaust ourselves day after day, year after year to attain proficiency.

Some experts have defined talent or genius as that which causes us to do the work and keep doing the work and keep working on our work to improve and make it better—not so much a gift of greatness but a gift that causes us to strive for greatness.

The bottom line is this—the onus is on us.

I am responsible for my life, for my work, as you are yours.

Apart from some notable exceptions and limitations, we set our ceilings, we define our cages.

I'm a far, far better novelist than I am a guitarist. I began working on the art and craft of novel writing twenty-four years before I began working on learning guitar. I wish I would've started playing guitar when I started writing novels—and I wish I would've started both at least a decade before I did. I wish I had known then what I know now, that everything takes work—and lots and lots of it. I wrongly thought some people had so-called natural talent in certain areas and others had it in other areas. But in seven or so years from now, if I'm still here, I will have been playing guitar for ten years and writing novels for nearly thirty-five, and I will be better at both than I am today, and I will be glad and grateful I started when I did.

Want the secret sauce recipe for success? Invest. Work. Commit. Keep learning and growing and evolving. Welcome feedback and criticism. Embrace failure as a trusted teacher. And never, ever stop. Keep at it. This is true of life itself, our relationships, and any endeavor we want to achieve.

What are you waiting for? Make a start today. Don't wait another second to make your beginning. It's going to require more time than you think you have, more energy, more work, more painful feedback and criticism, so suck it up, Buttercup, and get to it. You have deep within you the deep focus it takes to do the deep work required to achieve what you want to. The only question is: Will you?

# TWENTY-TWO

**Personal Aside**

AS MUCH AS I am stressing how vital deep focus is, as much as it has been proven to be a necessity for accomplishing great and important and difficult things, I have to say that throughout my career as a novelist, I have welcomed interruptions from my children. I have been only too happy for them to pull me out of my deep focus for the privilege of parenting them, of interacting with them often and on an ongoing basis.

This was true when they were small—and I was literally writing while bouncing them on my knee—and it is today when they are grown. Purposeful productivity is about doing what matters most. My children in particular and my family and friends in general are the biggest part of my priorities. Could I have done more and better work if I hadn't welcomed the interruptions to the process, hadn't integrated my writing into our lives and around their schedules? Without question. Would I change it? Only to increase the interruptions and time I get with them. Purposeful productivity isn't just about producing more, but producing more of what matters most, of having our best lives possible and getting the most we can out of them and sharing that with others. We must constantly guard against simple, hollow increased productivity lest we gain the whole world and lose our souls.

# TWENTY-THREE

**Don't Wait for Inspiration**

WRITER JACK LONDON SAID, "You can't wait for inspiration. You have to go after it with a club."

Spending time waiting for inspiration is wasted time.

Inspiration is a direct result of work, investment, practice.

You know what is far more important than inspiration? Your lifestyle.

Purposeful productivity is a way of living. It involves a certain mindset and mentality. It's a specific approach to life.

Your habits, routines, and practices, are far, far more important than inspiration, and actually lead to it.

Inspiration isn't something that happens to us. It's something we co-create with life—a lifestyle of deliberate, thoughtful work, openness and intentionality, and mindful creativity.

Because the so-called lightning bolts of inspiration often come to us when we least expect them, when we are thinking about or doing other things, we wrongly believe that inspiration is out of our control, something that happens to us instead of something we do.

But the way inspiration works is the result of a certain way of living and being creative, of working and being open. We have to form the right habits, routines, patterns, rituals, and to continually do the work with intentionality and openness before we can receive inspiration consistently.

Inspiration is the result of a certain way in which our minds work, particularly the subconscious part.

When we work hard and creatively, when we fill ourselves with knowledge and wisdom, then take a break, rest, or do something else, we give our subconscious minds time, space, and energy to not only figure out what we need but how to relay it to our conscious minds.

If you're working and get stuck, consider taking a nap, going for a walk, meditating, driving, showering, mowing the grass, or cleaning the house. Eventually, the answer will come to you.

This is the paradox of productivity. In order to be truly productive we have to take breaks, we have to have rest, we have to do other things. We wrongly think we can get more done by sticking with our work, by pressing through our fatigue and frustration, problems, and blockages, but most of the time it's the worst thing we can do. The mind is a wonderful slave but a terrible master. We too often attempt to do too much with our conscious minds and fail to use the vast, incredible resource of our subconscious minds.

Ironically, to be more productive you may need to work less —or at least differently.

When I first started writing fiction many years ago, I read as many books about the craft of writing as I could, and though I've long since forgotten most of what I read, certain concepts stuck with me—like this one from American author Norman

Mailer. He said that if a writer consistently sits down to write at the same time each day, she is essentially putting her subconscious on notice to prepare the material so that when she keeps the appointment the inspiration will be ready. I have found this to be true over the course of my career, and it's a powerful demonstration of the power of our subconscious minds. It also shows the relationship between routine and inspiration. Inspiration is a habit, a practice, a way of utilizing the subconscious mind.

YOU CAN EXPERIENCE CONSISTENT INSPIRATION —NOT by passively waiting for it, but by actively pursuing it, by doing your work and stepping back, as the Tao Te Ching teaches, by creating a symbiotic and synergistic relationship between your conscious and subconscious mind in your work. We must create systems, patterns, and habits conducive to inspiration, and continually practice them while living a lifestyle of openness and seeking.

We do not need to seek inspiration so much as live in a way that is conducive to inspiration. It has to do with being open and working hard. To have practices that create room for inspiration is a process, a lifestyle. Stop waiting for inspiration and start working the right way, and you'll have as much inspiration as you can handle.

**LIST YOUR WORK** routines and habits. Have you built in habits and practices that are conducive to inspiration? In what ways can you change your work patterns to allow for increased inspiration?

------------------------------------------------------------
------------------------------------------------------------
------------------------------------------------------------
------------------------------------------------------------
------------------------------------------------------------
------------------------------------------------------------


**I CAN'T STRESS** enough how important your routines and patterns and habits are. You have the power to create a life that leads to depth, richness, fullness, creativity, not just by the way you approach your life but by your approach to your work, by creating successful habits and routines, patterns and practices that lead to effectiveness and efficiency and inspiration.

# TWENTY-FOUR

**At Your Fingertips**

IN MY FIFTIETH year on the planet, following a catastrophic hurricane that turned my community into a post-apocalyptic landscape, I picked up the guitar.

I was told by several people who should know that it's not advisable to attempt to learn to play guitar later in life.

They weren't wrong. It wasn't easy, but I fell in love with playing and singing, and came to realize that it was something that had been missing from my life.

Since that fortunate day in October 2018 when I first borrowed my son's cheap acoustic guitar and started playing, I have practiced every single day since. It is often hard, sometimes painful work, but I find it more fun and fulfilling than I can say.

It's never too late for us to learn new things, to do new things, to do hard things, to discover or rediscover who and what we are meant to be and be doing. What are you waiting for? What's missing from your life?

I'm so grateful for the gift of music in general and the gift of guitar in particular.

I've picked up a lot of tips and tricks related to learning and playing over the years, and one of the most important is to keep your guitar out of its case and on a stand near you so that you can practice as often as possible.

If your instrument is visible and accessible, you will pick it up and play and practice far more than you would if it was tucked away in its case in the closet.

This same principle is why writers are encouraged to carry a notebook and a pen with them at all times.

Whatever you are pursuing, whatever your interests, whatever your passion, keep it close at hand, near your fingertips. Be able to access it at any moment, to actually be able to pick it up and practice it.

This leads to a level of productivity that's not possible any other way.

I actually purchased several inexpensive guitars and stands and placed them throughout my home house so I could practice even more—even if only for a few minutes at a time.

I've had more than a few people comment that it seems as though I have been playing longer than I have—and I have, but only because I've squeezed in more playing than I otherwise would, because my instrument is never far from my fingertips.

# TWENTY-FIVE

## The Little Things

ONE OF THE biggest mistakes I see people making when it comes to productivity is falsely believing that they have to wait until everything is optimal and they have a long periods of uninterrupted time to begin.

Our lives are made up of moments. We can fill each of these moments with the things that matter most to us, that are the most worth accomplishing, that we're most passionate about, or we can wait until we have the luxury of stringing many such moments together, which rarely ever happens.

If we're to be as productive as we possibly can and have the lives we really want, we must take advantage of the various free moments we have throughout each day instead of waiting until we have an extended period of time for our pursuits.

Early on in my novel writing career, I learned that it was far better for me to write at least a little every single day than to wait for longer stretches on weekends or holidays.

Everything we do, including writing a novel in my case, has momentum and energy. We keep that momentum going and continue to create energy by *doing*—and not just by doing but by doing consistently, on a regular, ongoing basis.

I've seen people complete projects by doing a little at a time while others are still waiting to find the perfect time to start.

Don't wait. Make a start during your next free moment. Fit in your passions and callings where you can. Be faithful over each moment you have and you will probably be rewarded with longer, more optimal times.

Stop self-sabotaging with the wrong mindset and approach.

If we write, we don't have to have the best computer and biggest office to do our work. If we play guitar, we don't have to have a world-class instrument, dedicated music room, and hours and hours of uninterrupted time. Perfect is the enemy of good. Perfectionism is a rehabilitating form of fear. Stop delaying. Start doing.

If you took advantage of the moments amiable to you and wrote just a single page per day, you'd be able to complete a book in a single year.

Except for a few rare occasions, I am usually ready to leave the house before my partner is—as was the case this fine Friday evening when we were going on a date for dinner and live music. Instead of merely waiting for her, instead of getting frustrated because she wasn't ready when she said she would be, I picked up my guitar and started practicing. Other times, I read a book, make notes, meditate, answer email, or put my clean clothes away—though this last not nearly often or timely enough. We only have so many moments allotted to us. What we do with each and every one matters. How foolish is it for us to waste a single one. And merely sitting and waiting for someone and fuming because they're late is a complete waste of those moments.

We can get far more done, far more out of life, if we see life as a series of moments and take advantage of those moments. It's a mistake to wait until we have long, extended periods of time to do something. Just as it is a mistake to wait until all our chores are done before we get to what matters most. If I listen to a book a few minutes at a time, I'm going to have read many more books when I reach the end of a week, a month, a year, or a lifetime than if I don't.

On the way back from our date, my partner and I stopped by the grocery store and picked up a few items we needed. Later, at home as I'm unloading the car and putting the groceries away, or even later as I'm brushing my teeth and preparing for bed, my partner will start laughing and say to me, "Are you listening to a book?"

She finds it funny, charming, and impressive (or at least she says she does) that I listen to an audiobook or a podcast any chance I get—even if, as is often the case, it's only for a few minutes at a time while unloading and putting away the groceries or brushing my teeth and peeing.

Don't waste this moment or any other. They are all we have.

# TWENTY-SIX

**Multitasking**

MULTITASKING HAS GOTTEN A BAD RAP—AND probably mostly deservedly so.

The important and complex things that matter most to us need our focus and concentration, need the full weight of our full attention.

But not everything requires the full weight of our full attention or our undivided focus. Certain necessary but non-taxing activities don't require much from us at all.

My practice of purposeful productivity has increased exponentially since I began grouping, batching, or multitasking certain tasks that can be done together, or done while doing other things.

The reality is that various parts of our brains are working simultaneously all the time. We are more than capable of multitasking. We're doing it right now. But certain tasks associated with our deepest work require deep, uninterrupted focus, require more of us, more of our minds, more of our attention, and knowing which those are and allocating them the resources they need is absolutely essential for purposeful productivity, for getting more out of our lives.

In my desire to get the most out of this one life I've been given, to not waste a single moment, I attempt to do more than one thing at a time when it's possible, practical, and advisable.

As I've mentioned, I'm almost always plotting my next novel, almost always trying to learn something new, almost always trying to connect with my children and loved ones. I'm often listening to an audiobook or a podcast, watching or listening to a Ted Talk or YouTube video while doing other things that don't require as much of me—such as exercising or cleaning or yard work or driving or showering.

These are moments that are ripe for increased productivity.

My partner often jokes that I never just brush my teeth or unload the car or clean the house or get my exercise but that I am always reading a book, learning something new, trying to grow and expand and evolve while doing those things. In fact, she suggested a possible title for this book might be *Brushing Your Teeth While Peeing*.

I recline and watch some TV late at night nearly every night. "Watching TV" is a misnomer. I don't have cable or satellite, so what I actually do is carefully curate what I watch and only watch that which interests, inspires, and entertains me. But I rarely just watch TV. Most often I am doing so with a guitar in my hands, practicing my chord shapes or fingerpicking patterns. I don't enjoy what I'm watching any less, and my guitar playing is improving much more quickly than it would be.

At any given moment, no matter what else I'm doing, I might also be checking email, organizing files, plotting a murder, doing Kegel exercises for sex or breathing exercises for singing, or meditating or thinking or exercising. So if we're talking and I get an odd look on my face, just say to yourself, *Is he doing Kegels or plotting a murder right now?*

If you search your life, you'll find a multiplicity of ways to increase your productivity. By doubling or tripling up on certain activities that are conducive to such an approach, we not only get more done but have more time to spend on the things that matter most—all of which leads to richer, fuller, more meaningful and fulfilling lives.

Look for ways that you can increase your productivity by combining activities.

What do you do each day that doesn't require your full focus and attention that would be conducive to adding an additional activity? Perhaps a far more meaningful, inspiring, or educational one.

Can you incorporate audiobooks and podcasts and YouTube videos and other forms of learning into your exercise routines or into your hygiene routines or into your household chores?

# TWENTY-SEVEN

**Habits**

FOR BETTER OR WORSE, for good or ill, the reality is that I am my habits and you are yours.

Many of them are helpful and beneficial, but some are not only killing our productivity but sabotaging our quality of life.

We're aware of many of them, but there may be just as many that we're completely clueless about.

A habit is a settled or regular tendency or practice, an often automatic behavior, especially one that is hard to give up.

Habits can be helpful or harmful, and we can take steps to create and consciously cultivate healthy ones while eliminating harmful ones.

Our productivity, our success, the quality of our lives are dependent upon our habits—perhaps more than anything else.

Habits, routines, systems, discipline, and ingrained behaviors work when all else fails.

Prior to the summer of 1994, I didn't have a daily habit of

writing. But that summer I developed one—by setting a schedule and sticking to it, by practicing over and over and over the behavior that I wanted to become a habit. Since that summer, I've written nearly every day, and the days that I am unable to leave me feeling frustrated and incomplete.

Before the fall of 2018, I didn't play the guitar. But during that October following the catastrophic Cat 5 hurricane that decimated our region, I formed a habit—through repeated action—and I've played every day since then. Now I feel frustrated when I don't get to practice and play as much as I would like.

For nearly all of my life, I have played basketball and lifted weights about every other day. My body feels best when I'm active, when my muscles have been stretched and worked. Of course, exercise doesn't just make my body feel good. It has an enormously positive effect on my mind, on my thoughts and emotions as well. My activities related to playing basketball and lifting weights are habits I formed in childhood and adolescence that have served me well throughout adulthood.

Desire to do something must be accompanied by the discipline to actually do it, but done long enough, the discipline is replaced by more desire.

Repetitive thoughts become obsessive. Repetitive actions become habitual.

We get good at what we do repeatedly.

We are what we do.

Habits can be among the most helpful and efficient actions we take. They can lead us directly to accomplishing our goals or they can sabotage us and lead us directly away from our purpose.

The strength and weakness of habits is in how thoughtlessly they can be accomplished. They are shortcuts, automatons, autopilot-type sequences that are meant to save time and energy and effort. But this automatic part is what makes them so dangerous. In general, we are at our best when we're aware of what we're doing, when we're fully awake to our thoughts, our actions, and their consequences.

One solution to help decrease our bad habits and increase the meaning and efficiency of our good ones is to add mindfulness to everything we do. Do our best to end our automatic and thoughtless responses and actions, and raise our awareness of exactly what our mentality and mindset, words, and actions are.

I am my habits—both good and bad.

I am more than my habits, of course, but I wonder just how much more than our habits we can be. What if our bad habits are jesses—the strong leather straps tied around falcons' ankles by falconers to control them? As we attempt to soar, is it our bad habits that keep us tethered to the ground?

I have many bad habits—some of which I'm working on, some I haven't even begun to tackle yet, others I'm not even aware of, though my commitment is to become aware as soon as possible.

I have bad habits of eating way too much sugar and snacking late at night. And the only reason I still have these habits is because I've not made the decision to break them, to do the work of undoing these habits and replacing them with better, more beneficial ones. The same is true for all the bad habits I persist in.

Let's say I wanted to break my bad habit of sugar consumption and late-night snacking. What should I do?

A good place to begin is with my mind. What are the thoughts that lead to this behavior? What perceived need is being met? Why do I persist in doing something that is bad for me? Examining what's happening in my mind and addressing it is definitely a good place to start.

Then I need to put myself in situations and circumstances that will give me my best chance of success—such as quit keeping so many Reese's in the house, replacing them instead with healthier snacks.

Another strategy I could employ is sandwiching a new habit between two established good habits, allowing them to give structure to and support the new habit. After all, without the bread it's not a sandwich. It's just a sad, lonely piece of bologna meat.

Next I need to take these right actions repeatedly until they become habitual—likely for several weeks or even months.

Finally, I might also consider rewarding myself for my small successes. In general, I want to be internally, intrinsically motivated, but perhaps a little external motivation as I'm trying to build new habits might not be such a bad thing.

Few things we do will determine our productivity, success, and the satisfaction of our lives like our habits. Any investment we make in better habits will pay enormous dividends, particularly over our lifetimes.

# TWENTY-EIGHT

**Editing and Iteration**

I'VE LEARNED a lot about life through my practice of writing.

One of the most essential concepts I've learned is the importance of editing and iterating.

Novelist and writer Ernest Hemingway said, "The first draft of anything is shit."

That's relative, of course, but he's right. Our first drafts can be improved upon, can be made better, need editing and iterating. This is true no matter what you and I do. Whatever it is, we can always make it better. It is only through editing and iterating, continuously improving that we can get anywhere close to the pristine perfection of our original dream or vision.

There are no shortcuts.

If we're going to be good at life, if we're going to be productive, if we're going to master what matters most to us, we must continuously be investing and working and editing and iterating.

To start, it's critical that we use critical thinking to evaluate everything we do. It's critical that we receive feedback and input from trusted others who have mastered what we are attempting to achieve.

Once we have subjected ourselves, our lives and relationships, and our work to critical thinking and honest feedback, we must then take the next step and apply it. This is editing. This is iterating. This is our only opportunity to become prolific and proficient, to attain the excellence that is not automatic, and it only comes through practicing, editing, and iterating.

For this to happen requires an ego death, an end to closed defensiveness, and a commitment to improvement above all else.

Rumi said, "If you are irritated by every rub, how will your mirror be polished?"

Egoic defensiveness of our work, of our actions, of our selves prevents the growth and mastery that comes from embracing the editing and iterating process.

One of the things I learned early on in novel-writing workshops was how vital a writer's commitment to improving the work was. If it wasn't prioritized above all else, the work would never improve. Week after week I watched as writers defended themselves against the criticism they were receiving—explaining what they really meant or why their work can't be improved upon instead of openly hearing the feedback being offered.

As long as these writers took this approach, their work didn't improve.

If my goal as a writer is for my novel to be the best it can be, I will welcome the suggestions and input of others and apply their perspectives, reactions, and criticisms as I edit and rewrite.

If instead my commitment is to defend my work and guard my ego, to take as a personal affront any criticism I receive, then I will never improve, never get better, never reach my potential.

This is true of every aspect of our beings and every facet of our lives. And, in fact, life continuously gives us opportunities to question, to listen, to receive, to edit and iterate.

One of the ways we can become more productive today is to check our egos and commit ourselves to the arduous and sometimes painful process of editing and iterating.

The only way you and I will ever attain any type of excellence in life and work is through commitment to constant improvement.

No person is ever complete or perfect. No work is ever finished.

The novels I write and the songs I play today are better than the ones I did twenty or two years ago—but only because of practice, openness to feedback, editing and iterating—and they both have much, much room for improvement.

Everything we do is a relative failure, is incomplete and imperfect, and our goal should be to continually fail better. Suck a little less.

If everything we do is a relative failure, then it is a relative success too, and we can focus only on that part, find our solace and worth by seeing only the good, pat ourselves on the head like good little pups for what we did right. This may or may not be a valid life choice—you have to decide for yourself—but it absolutely will not lead to the improvement that only editing and iterating can achieve.

The choice is simple really—pretend we're perfect and give ourselves a pat, or know we're not, open ourselves to criticism, and commit ourselves to editing and iterating.

# TWENTY-NINE

## The Pareto Principle

YOU'RE familiar with Vilfredo Pareto's observation whether you know that's what it's called or not. As an economist in the early twentieth century, Pareto realized that 80 percent of the land in Italy was owned by 20 percent of the people. He ultimately went on to apply this 80/20 observation not only to other countries but other aspects of life and work.

Today his principle is popularly known as the 80/20 rule. And the point of it for our purposes here is this—20 percent of your actions will result in 80 percent of what you produce.

It's not exact, of course, but some small percentage of your work will yield the largest portion of your productivity.

Want to be more productive? Want to work smarter, be more efficient? Examine what you do and what results from it. Look at it closely and carefully. Determine which of your activities result in a disproportionate amount of what you produce. Once you've identified your actions and activities that yield the greatest results, then do more of them. Begin to use more than 20 percent of your time and energy on those things that are producing more. By doing a little math and reallocating some resources, your productivity will increase exponentially.

If 20 percent of our actions produce 80 percent of the results, we'd be foolish not to examine why and attempt to do even more of these 20 percent activities and ultimately increase our productivity. The truth is it's probably not 80/20. It could be 90/10 or 70/30. The percentages aren't nearly as important as the principle. If you look closely enough, you will find that a small percentage of the things you do are vitally important to your productivity and a large percentage are not important at all.

THE KEY IS for us to find out what is working and what is not. Then to do less of what's not working and more of what is.

Let's say you own a few stocks. If the shares you have in the ACME Corporation are outperforming the shares you have in all other companies combined, shouldn't you sell the other shares and invest even more into ACME?

Double down on what's working. Stop trying to force something to work that isn't.

This approach requires us to experiment and to fail. We won't know what works and what doesn't until we actually try. Failing is essential. We should embrace it—not in the sense that we won't stop failing at something once we've begun, but in its necessity to show us where to and where not to allocate our valuable, limited, precious resources.

Want to know the secret to success? Do more of what works and less of what doesn't.

Of course, this requires trial and error, honest examination, and the strength, wisdom, and grace to double down on certain actions and activities while jettisoning others.

Perhaps we'd rather not climb up on the bathroom scales each morning. Perhaps we'd rather not take a close look and careful evaluation of our lives, our relationships, our thoughts, our actions, our words, our work. Nobody's going to make us. It's entirely up to us. Most people don't. Most of us in this mad, mad world cling to the insanity of continuing with the same attitudes and actions while expecting a different result.

You and I only get 100 percent of our lives—however long that winds up being. We can't increase that, can't go over 100, but we can change, alter, edit, iterate, and reallocate what we do with the various percentages that make up that 100—and beginning with Pareto's 80/20 principle is a great place to start.

# THIRTY

**Today**

I BLINK open my eyes and am excited to start the day.

As a novelist, I mostly set my own schedule and have the luxury of freedom and flexibility. I go to bed when I get sleepy and sleep until I wake up—and have done with very few exceptions over the past twenty-plus years of my writing career.

Of the many thrilling reasons to greet the day with enthusiasm and expectation, to find out what happens next in the novel I'm writing is very high on the list.

Today, like every day, there's so much I want to do, to experience, to learn, to become.

The relentless clock inside my head is counting down, each tick echoing ever closer to my deadline of deadlines.

I am acutely aware of how short my time is, of how this is the only one of these days I will get.

How often I wish I could, like the character of Phil the weatherman from the movie *Groundhog Day*, relive over and over so many of my days. But this, like the wish for more wishes, has so far gone ungranted by a genie.

Many mornings I rush straight to my writing chair and the keyboard waiting for me there to write my morning pages, but today I stop by my other desk first. This is not a best practice. Before starting my work on my novel, I check email, check my bank balances, and watch some of the coverage of the basketball game from the night before. As I do these things, I do some eye exercises, some Kegels, some finger and knee physical therapy with a couple of other health treatments.

My work—both its quality and quantity—would be better served if I had skipped this step and, still sleepy, directly entered the world of my fictive dream, but, hey, I'm not a machine. I'm not always my best most productive self. What I'm doing is not a waste of time. It would just be better if I did it at another time of the day—after my word work was done.

This afternoon I'll be keeping Autumn, my little four-year-old buddy who I help watch while her mom's at work, so I have a chunk of time to get things done this morning before I pick her up.

I want to spend time with my children, my new grandchild, and other loved ones today. I want to write. I want to meditate, reflect, journal, and think. I want to exercise and work out. I want to practice some guitar and singing. I want to play basketball. I want to read and listen to a podcast. I want to fit in plenty of fun, play, and R&R, and about a thousand other things.

As I create my to-do list today, I divide it up into what I need to do before I pick up Autumn, what I might be able to do while she's here, and what I'll do this evening after she is gone.

It's possible to fit in my workout in between playing with and caring for Autumn. I can probably also do some of my household chores while she is eating or watching a video. But I need to get my writing done before and after she is here—mostly before, when my brain is at its best.

I sit in my writing chair and, because of routine and habit and preparation, begin writing immediately and am quickly in the deep-focus zone. The words flow and I make the most of the hours I have. Other days I will have more time. I will write and break and write and break, but today I have one session and I have to get as much done as I possibly can.

Many of the best and most important things we do in life need our complete and full attention. I get lost in the present moment of creation as the words pour out of me in the same way I get lost as Autumn pretends we are good and bad princesses in a castle in a kingdom far away or a square sponge who lives in a pineapple at the bottom of the sea.

I wrap up my writing with about half an hour until I pick up Autumn, so quickly grab my guitar and practice playing and singing a few songs. I might be able to fit in a little guitar practice while she's here, but I won't be able to play and sing entire songs, so I use this half-hour to go over a few of the songs that need the most work.

Autumn and I always have fun together. We play with her toys. We play pretend and make up games. We go to the park. We go swimming. We jump on the trampoline. We play hide and seek and chase. We watch videos of other kids playing and cartoons. Autumn, like my other loved ones, is a priority, and I'm happy to fit my work in around her, to maximize the time I get with her.

Caring for a small child is demanding—especially when giving them your full attention—but throughout the day, while Autumn is here and when she's not, I look for ways to add meaning and value to this extraordinary gift of life I've been given. In a given moment, taking a deep breath, slowing down, and taking life in brings calmness and invokes the sacred.

Reading a few lines of poetry or prose, gazing at the art on my wall or the lake beyond the cypress trees in my backyard enhances my experience of these priceless moments.

In between caring for and playing with Autumn, I might check email, make notes for my novel—especially the solution my subconscious just gave me as I was doing something else—write a few lines of prose, jot down some possible song lyrics, do some research, pick up my guitar and practice because it's on a stand beside my desk, check in with my loved ones via text or a quick phone call, fit in a little cleaning, gather and take out the trash, or many other things. But I mostly hang with Autumn.

I live in a small town. All the shops and stores are close by. All of my loved ones live minutes away. This saves tons of time and enables me to get more done and be more productive. Today as I walk uptown to get a haircut, I listen to and work on a new song I'm trying to learn on the guitar. If I had brought my earbuds I could have continued to listen to the song inside the salon while I was wait, but I forgot them so I read an article on my phone and visit with the stylists instead.

There's a pick-up basketball at the old gym tonight and I plan on playing. However, lately on this particular night of the week the crowds showing up to play are huge. So instead of wasting a lot of time sitting around waiting to play in between games, I invite a few of the guys to come early to play before everyone else arrives. The way we play is that the winning team stays on the court, so when the others arrive and we start playing, I will play until I lose and then leave. If there happens to be a smaller group tonight and none of us have to sit for more than one game at a time, I'll stay longer. But either way I get my workout in without wasting a lot of time waiting.

When I return from playing basketball, my partner and I have dinner together—talking and hanging out as we prepare it and then sitting down together to eat it. Following dinner, we grab our instruments and practice some songs for an upcoming gig we have. Then later in the evening when we are ready to relax, we sit on the loveseat in our media room and watch TV—usually some inspirational, educational YouTube videos, some basketball games, some true crime documentaries, or some mystery suspense shows, these last for ideas and inspiration for my next novel. I'm always in research mode, always looking for the next idea, so do most everything with this in mind.

As we sit and watch, talk, and hang, I have my guitar and am practicing quietly but persistently. Of course, I put down the instrument from time to time so that we can hold hands, cuddle, snuggle, or run to the kitchen and get snacks.

Nearly every night my partner goes to bed before I do, so after tucking her in, I either relax some more, do some more research, practice some more guitar, or, if I have the brain cells and bandwidth left to do so, work on my novel some more.

I often spend time during this period late at night thinking, contemplating, reflecting, journaling, processing, and preparing for the following day.

When I get sleepy or just feel like it's time to lie down and try to go to sleep, I listen to an audiobook or a podcast with headphones unless I need to think or process or meditate or work on character and plot ideas.

And then, as the day ends for my conscious mind, my subconscious gets to be its most productive, toiling in the underworld of what dreams may come.

And then . . .

Wake. Rinse. Repeat.

# THIRTY-ONE

## MORE

THE THINGS that matter most to me are:

------------------------------------------------
------------------------------------------------
------------------------------------------------
------------------------------------------------
------------------------------------------------
------------------------------------------------
------------------------------------------------
------------------------------------------------
------------------------------------------------
------------------------------------------------
------------------------------------------------

I WOULD LIKE my obituary to say:

_____
_____
_____
_____
_____
_____

THE THINGS that give my life the most purpose, meaning, fulfillment, and satisfaction are:

_____
_____
_____
_____
_____
_____

WHY AM I not doing more of these things?

_____
_____
_____
_____
_____
_____

HOW COULD I be doing more of these things?

_____
_____
_____
_____
_____
_____

HAVE I organized and prioritized my life and work, my workspace and workflow? If not, what am I waiting for? Be honest.

_____
_____
_____
_____
_____
_____

DO I HAVE A MISSION STATEMENT? Lifelong goals? Yearly goals? Am I working from daily, weekly, monthly lists? If not, why not?

_____
_____
_____
_____
_____
_____

AM I going after inspiration with a club? Am I scheduling time for my subconscious mind to work its magic? If not, what am I waiting for?

_____
_____
_____
_____
_____
_____

AM I decreasing the space between the things that matter most? How could I do this more?

_____
_____
_____
_____
_____
_____

AM I multitasking the things I can? Am I deeply focusing on the things that are the most important and require the most from me? How can I do more of each?

---

HOW HAVE I been editing and iterating my life and work? What are some areas I can do more?

---

AM I BUILDING BETTER HABITS? Am I replacing bad habits with better ones? If not, why? If so, how could I replace more bad habits with good ones?

---------------------------------------------------------------
---------------------------------------------------------------
---------------------------------------------------------------
---------------------------------------------------------------
---------------------------------------------------------------
---------------------------------------------------------------

HAVE I examined my life and work from the standpoint of the 80/20 principle? Have I attempted to allocate more resources to the 20 percent?

---------------------------------------------------------------
---------------------------------------------------------------
---------------------------------------------------------------
---------------------------------------------------------------
---------------------------------------------------------------
---------------------------------------------------------------

# THE MORE GUIDED JOURNAL

Don't miss the MORE Guided Journal

# THE MEANING SERIES

MORE is part of the Meaning Series by Michael Lister. Check out the other informative and inspirational titles today.

www.ingramcontent.com/pod-product-compliance
Lightning Source LLC
Chambersburg PA
CBHW030335100526
44592CB00010B/702